History's Greatest Commanders

CHILDREN'S MILITARY & WAR HISTORY BOOKS

BABY PROFESSOR

EDUCATION KIDS

Speedy Publishing LLC

40 E. Main St. #1156

Newark, DE 19711

www.speedypublishing.com

Copyright 2016

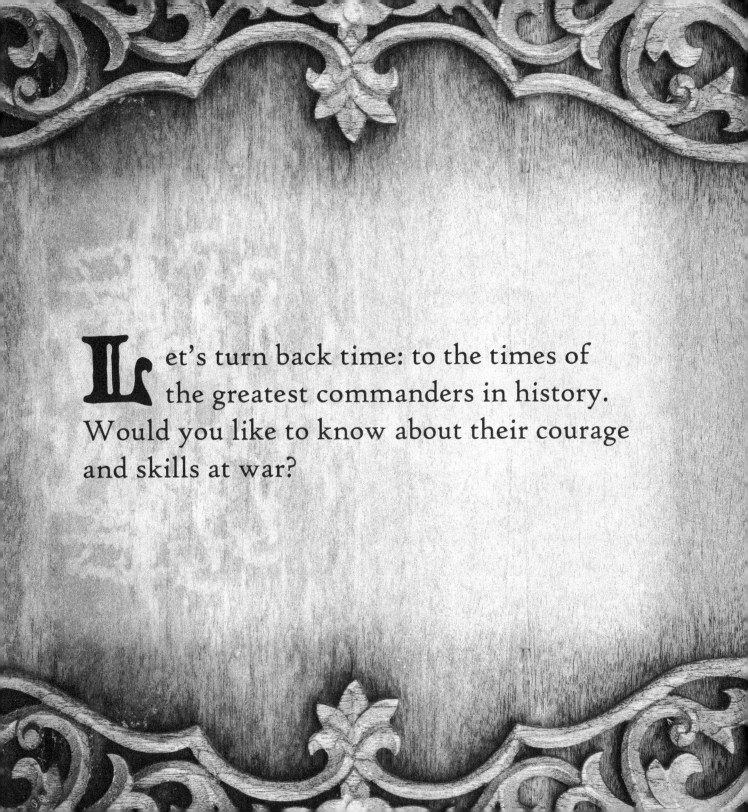

Let's turn back time: to the times of the greatest commanders in history. Would you like to know about their courage and skills at war?

The greatest commanders in the world's history won great battles and defeated their enemies. They served as inspiration to their soldiers.

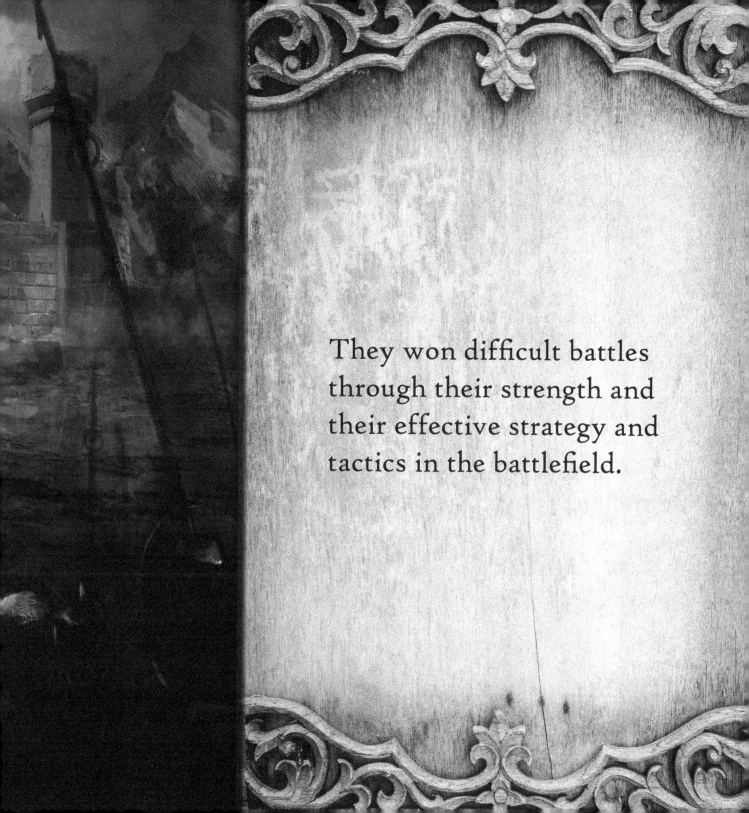

They won difficult battles through their strength and their effective strategy and tactics in the battlefield.

Their courage is praised by historians and citizens of the world across all ages. These men at war from long ago are still remembered today.

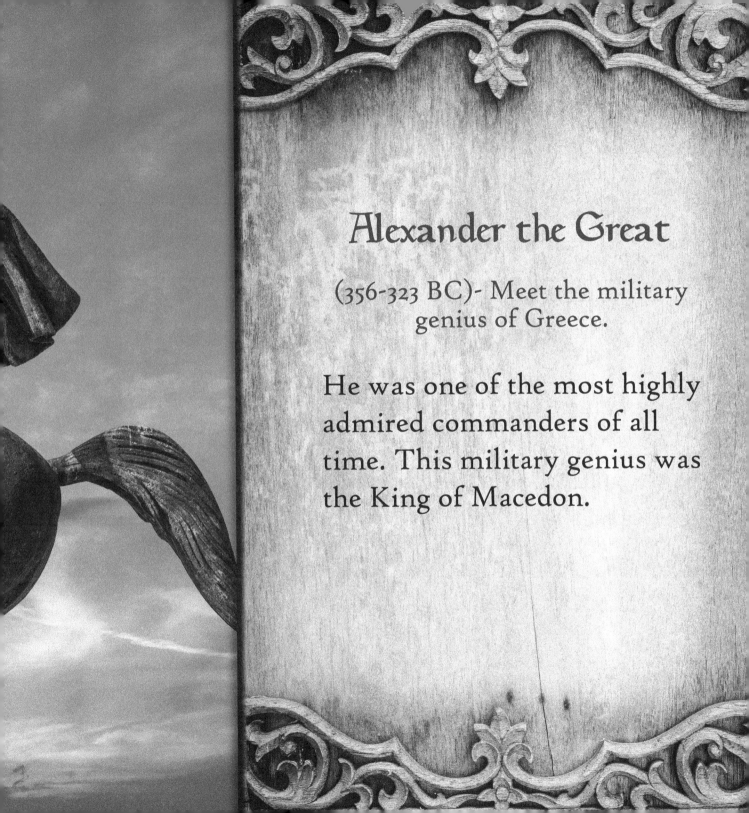

Alexander the Great

(356-323 BC)- Meet the military genius of Greece.

He was one of the most highly admired commanders of all time. This military genius was the King of Macedon.

He became king after the assassination of his father, when Alexander was very young. He led armies of 50,000 soldiers in a mission of expanding his territory and the kingdom.

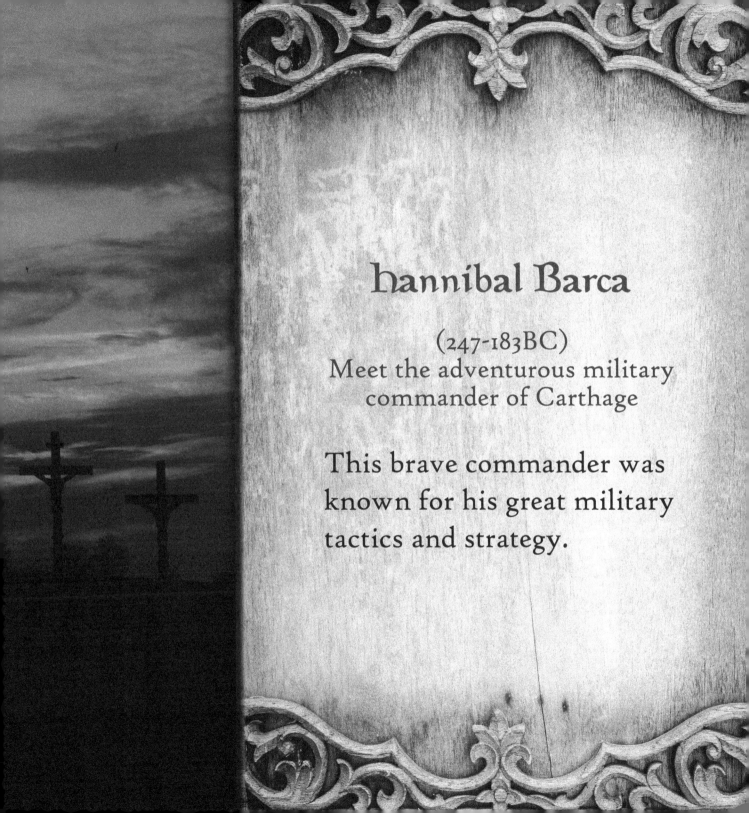

hannibal Barca

(247-183BC)
Meet the adventurous military
commander of Carthage

This brave commander was
known for his great military
tactics and strategy.

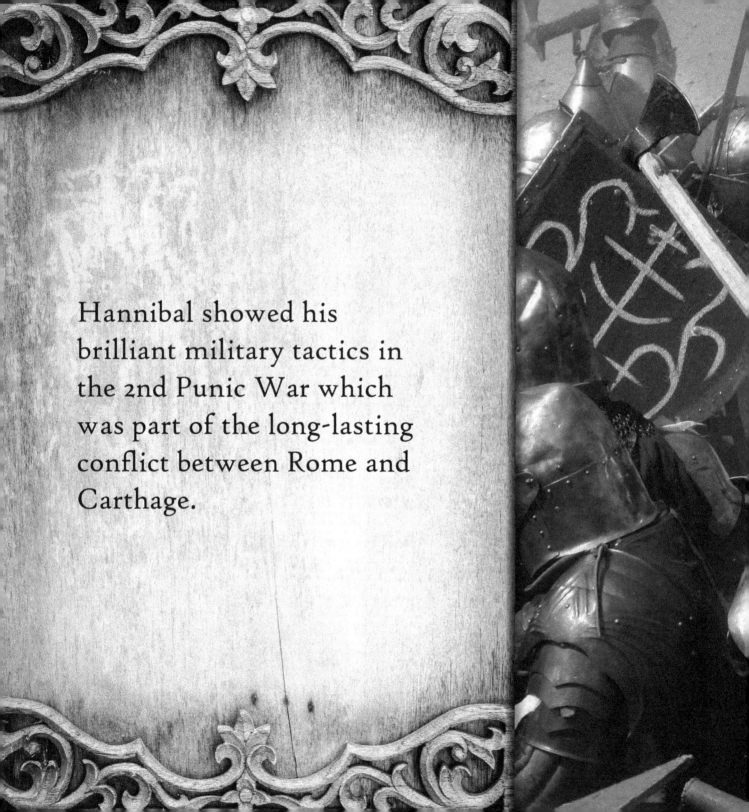

Hannibal showed his brilliant military tactics in the 2nd Punic War which was part of the long-lasting conflict between Rome and Carthage.

However, despite his great military strategy his mission to conquer Rome failed, and he committed suicide.

Cyrus the Great

(590-580BC)
Meet the First King of the
Persian Empire

Cyrus led the Persians to
conquer the Medes. For
the first time in history, he
unified all of what is now
Iran. One of his visions
was to establish the largest
empire in the world.

He was indeed great as a leader, for, beside his military victories, he issued the first human rights concepts in the ancient world. Inhabitants of Persia were allowed to exercise many rights.

Julius Caesar

(100-54 BC)
Meet the Brilliant Roman
Emperor

He was a great general,
lawgiver, builder and
politician. Julius Caesar
was one of the most famous
figures in ancient times. His
unparalleled influence had
an impact on the ancient as
well as the modern world.

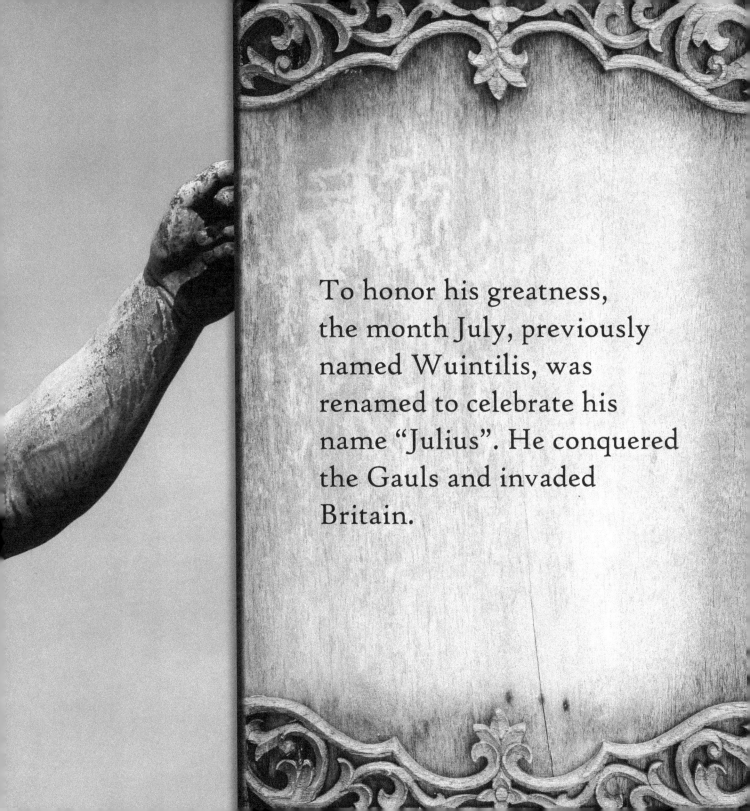

To honor his greatness, the month July, previously named Wuintilis, was renamed to celebrate his name "Julius". He conquered the Gauls and invaded Britain.

Sun Tzu

(544-496 BC)
Meet the Chinese Military General

He was a great war strategist. He authored the book "The Art of War", which changed how war was fought in ancient times.

Many military commanders and nations followed his book, which even influenced in European and American soldiers and leaders in the 20th century.

Napoleon Bonaparte

Meet the General of the French Revolution

This great man rose through the tumult of the French Revolution and created a new French empire with himself as Emperor. He conquered much of Europe and created a new code of civil laws.

Leonidas

(540-480 BC) Meet the
Military King of Sparta

He was best admired
for his extraordinary
performance on the Battle
of Thermopylae. With his
small yet strong force, he
fought against the huge
army of Xerxes.

Trajan

53AD-17 AD
Meet the Great Roman
Military Warrior

He became famous when
he conquered Dacia, the
modern-day Romania and
Moldova. He also defeated
the Parthians. He created
a new province after he
conquered Mesopotamia.

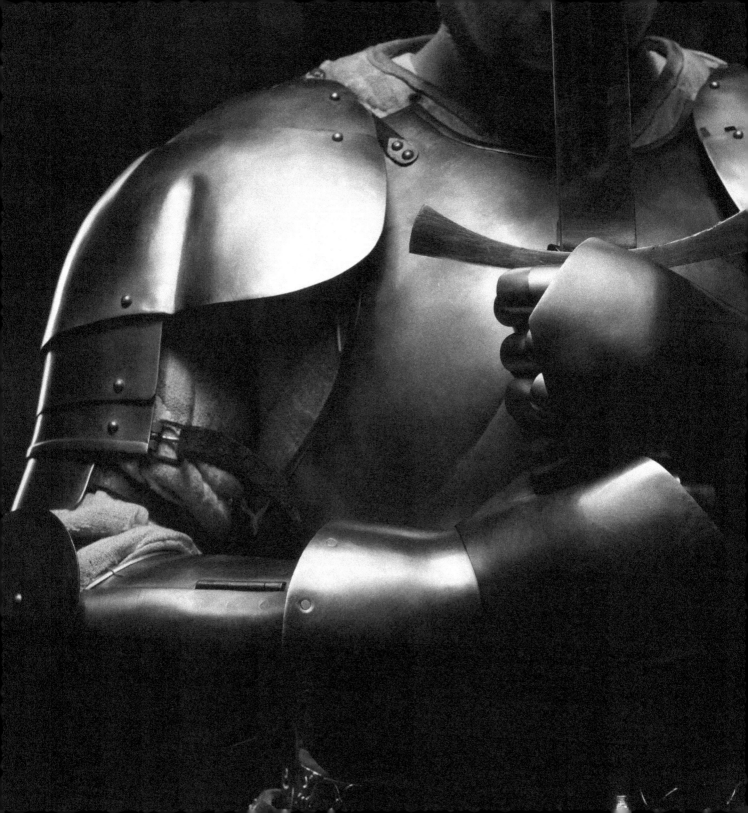

These great commanders in history achieved amazing successes in war through their brilliant military knowledge and strategies.

Visit

BABY PROFESSOR
EDUCATION KIDS

www.BabyProfessorBooks.com

to download Free Baby Professor eBooks
and view our catalog of new and exciting
Children's Books

CPSIA information can be obtained
at www.ICGtesting.com
Printed in the USA
BVHW060338300622
640934BV00006B/629

9 781541 902008